EXPLODING EXPERIMENTS FOR EXCEPTIONAL LEARNERS

SCIENCE BOOK FOR KIDS 9-12

CHILDREN'S SCIENCE EDUCATION BOOKS

Speedy Publishing LLC

40 E. Main St. #1156

Newark, DE 19711

www.speedypublishing.com

Copyright 2017

In this book, we're going to talk about doing some fun experiments where things explode. So, let's get right to it!

You can do some fun experiments with things that explode with just a few basic supplies. Make sure there's always an adult helping you when you do science experiments!

EXPERIMENT 1

FANTASTIC FOAM

THINGS YOU'LL NEED:

You'll need a clean, empty soda bottle made of plastic, 16-ounce size. You'll also need ½ cup of 20-volume solution of hydrogen peroxide. For the hydrogen peroxide, you need to have a solution of 6%, so make sure an adult gets this for you from a hair salon or store that sells beauty supplies. It's important for it be a 6% solution. You'll also need 1 package of yeast that's dry, which is about a tablespoon of yeast, 3 measuring tablespoons of hot water to activate the yeast, some liquid dishwashing soap, some food coloring, a small cup, and some safety goggles to wear. You might need a small funnel too.

WHAT TO DO:

Explosions make a mess so make sure to place your supplies on a tray or washable surface.

Hydrogen peroxide liquid can irritate your eyes or your skin, so be sure to put the safety goggles on. Have the adult who is helping you pour the ½ cup of liquid 6% solution into the soda bottle.

Add about 8 droplets of food dye into the hydrogen peroxide. You can use any color you want!

Add about 1 tablespoon of soap, the liquid dishwashing type, into the mixture and shake the bottle a little to combine it.

In a cup, stir together the warm water with the contents of the dry yeast packet. Mix it for about ½ a minute.

Now the fun starts! Use a funnel to pour the mixture of yeast into the soda bottle. Watch the awesome foaminess!

THE SCIENCE BEHIND IT:

You just created an exothermic reaction. The chemical reaction you created produced a lot of foam and it also created some heat. You may have noticed that the bottle got warm. The yeast is a catalyst, which simply means it helped the reaction along. The yeast removed the element of oxygen from the peroxide creating a super foamy mixture of water, oxygen, and soap. Each bubble in the foam is filled with oxygen. You can clean up the foam with a sponge. Make sure to pour any leftover liquid down the drain with some water.

Some people call this demonstration "elephant's toothpaste" because it looks like a huge amount of toothpaste coming out of a tube. Don't put any of the foam in your mouth though! It's not safe to eat or drink.

500
400
500 мл
300
200

EXPERIMENT 2

MY LUNCH BAG JUST EXPLODED!

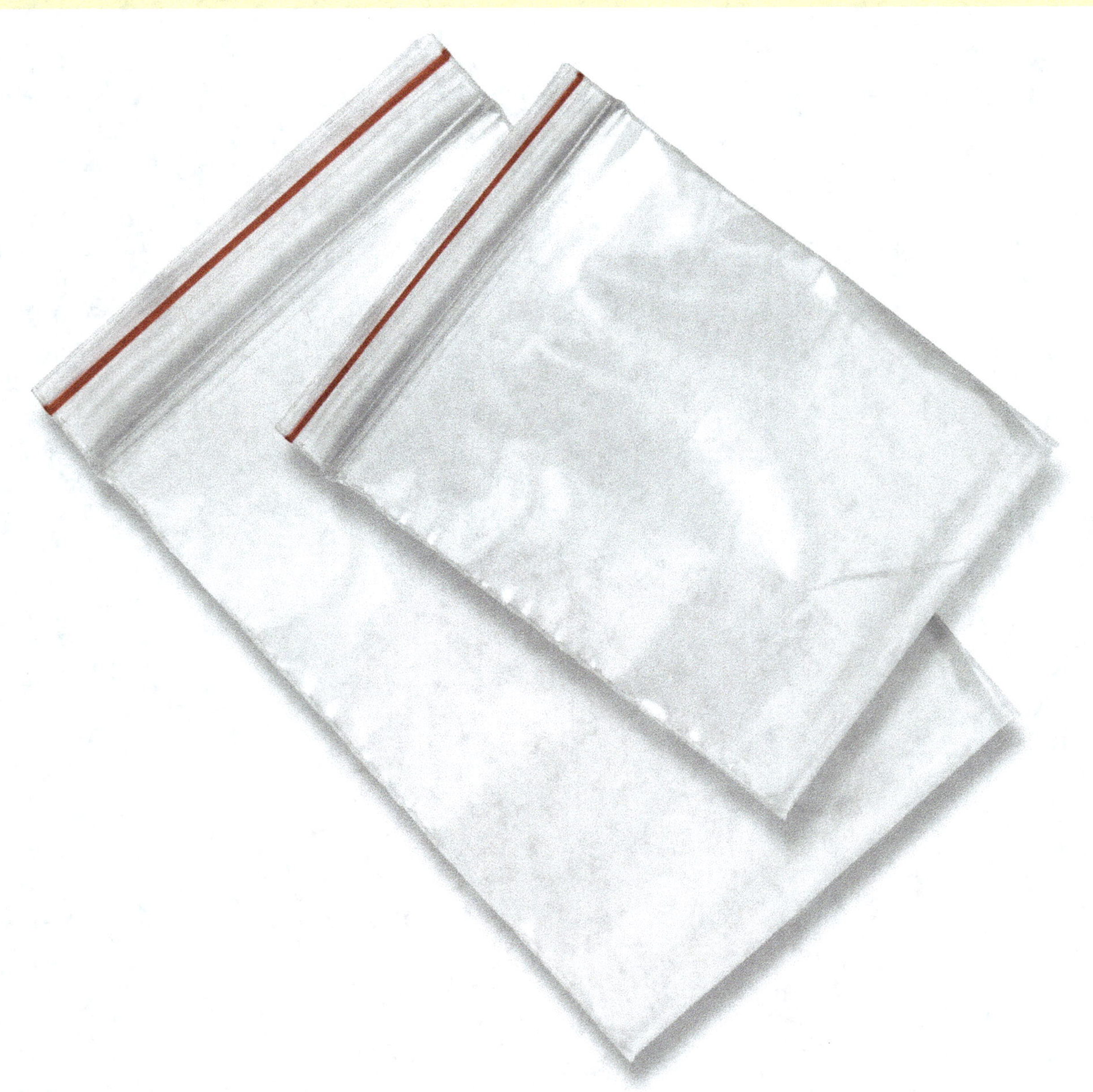

THINGS YOU'LL NEED:

You'll need a small zip-lock type bag. A freezer bag that is sandwich-sized works best. You'll also need some baking soda, some warm water, some white vinegar, measuring cups, measuring spoons, and a small tissue.

WHAT TO DO:

You should probably go outside to do this experiment.

Place about ¼ cup of scalding hot water into the bag.

Place about ½ cup of vinegar to the hot water that's in the bag.

Put 1 tablespoon of baking soda inside the middle of a tissue. Fold the sides of the tissue up like a package so the white powder doesn't spill out.

STEP 5

This part has to be done fast. Zip the bag so it's partially closed. Just leave enough space open so you can throw in your tissue packet with the white powder. Throw the packet into the zip-lock bag and close it up tight.

STEP 6

Put the bag down on the ground in your backyard and step away. If you've done everything right, the bag will start expanding and then it might even explode with a pop!

vinegar
baking
soda

THE SCIENCE BEHIND IT:

You created an Acid-Base chemical reaction! When the baking soda and vinegar mix they created carbon dioxide. That's the gas that we breathe out when we breathe. Gases need a lot of space to expand so the carbon dioxide starts filling the bag and when it doesn't have any more space it goes POP! Be sure to clean everything up and recycle the leftover plastic.

EXPERIMENT 3

BLAST-OFF ROCKET

THINGS YOU'LL NEED:

You're going to need some safety goggles. You're also going to need an empty 35 mm plastic camera film holder and lid. These aren't easy to find anymore because people rarely use these to hold film since most people have digital cameras now. The plastic white canisters work better than the ones that are black. You'll need to ask your parents or your adult supervisor for an antacid tablet, such as Alka-Seltzer. You'll also need some water.

WHAT TO DO:

STEP 1

Go outside for this experiment. This "rocket" is going to take off! Be sure to put on your safety goggles.

STEP 2

Break the Alka-Seltzer tablet in half.

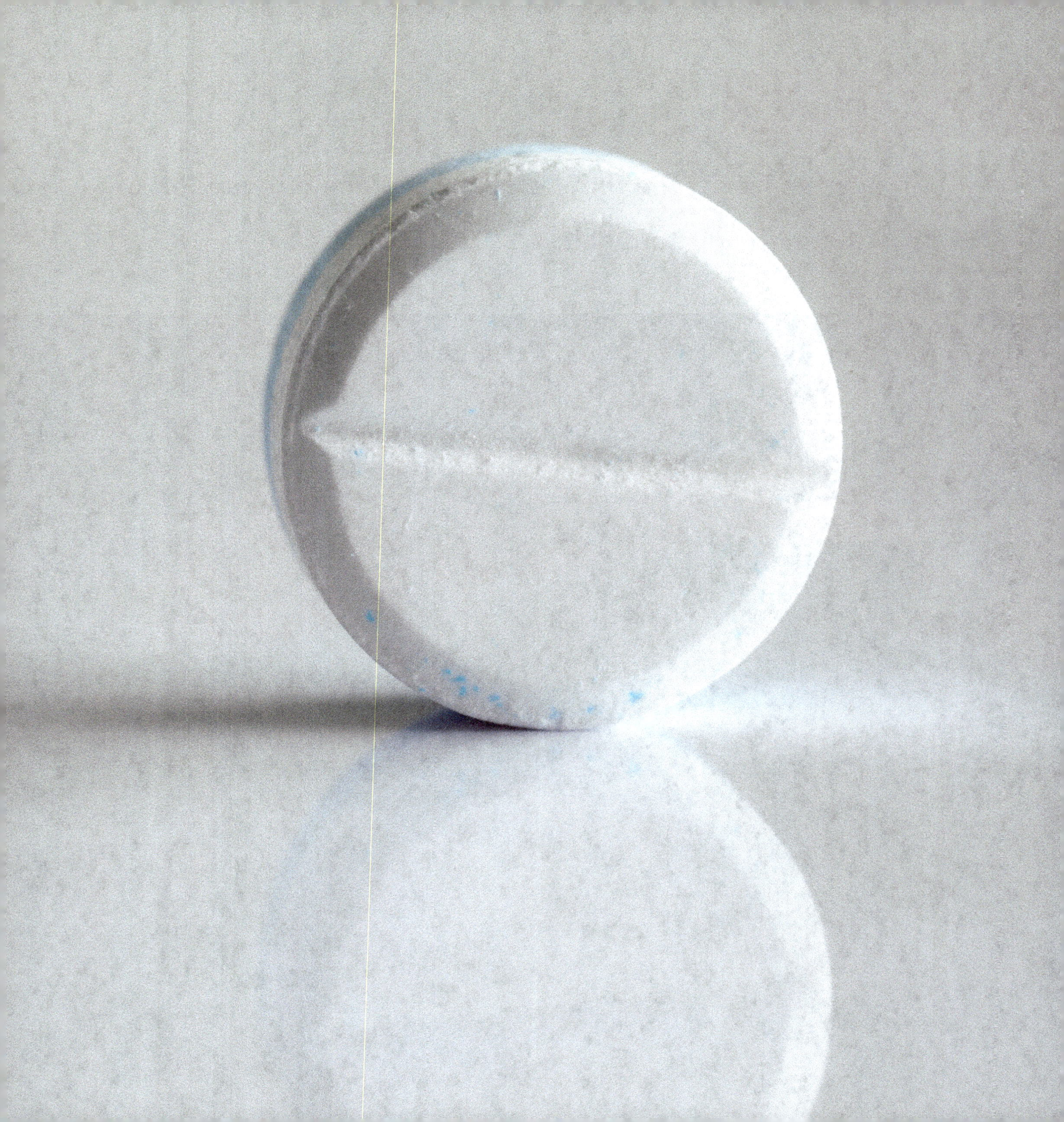

Take the lid off the film holder and place a teaspoon of water in the bottom of it.

You'll have to act fast on the next few steps. Drop the half tablet into the film holder and snap the lid on tight.

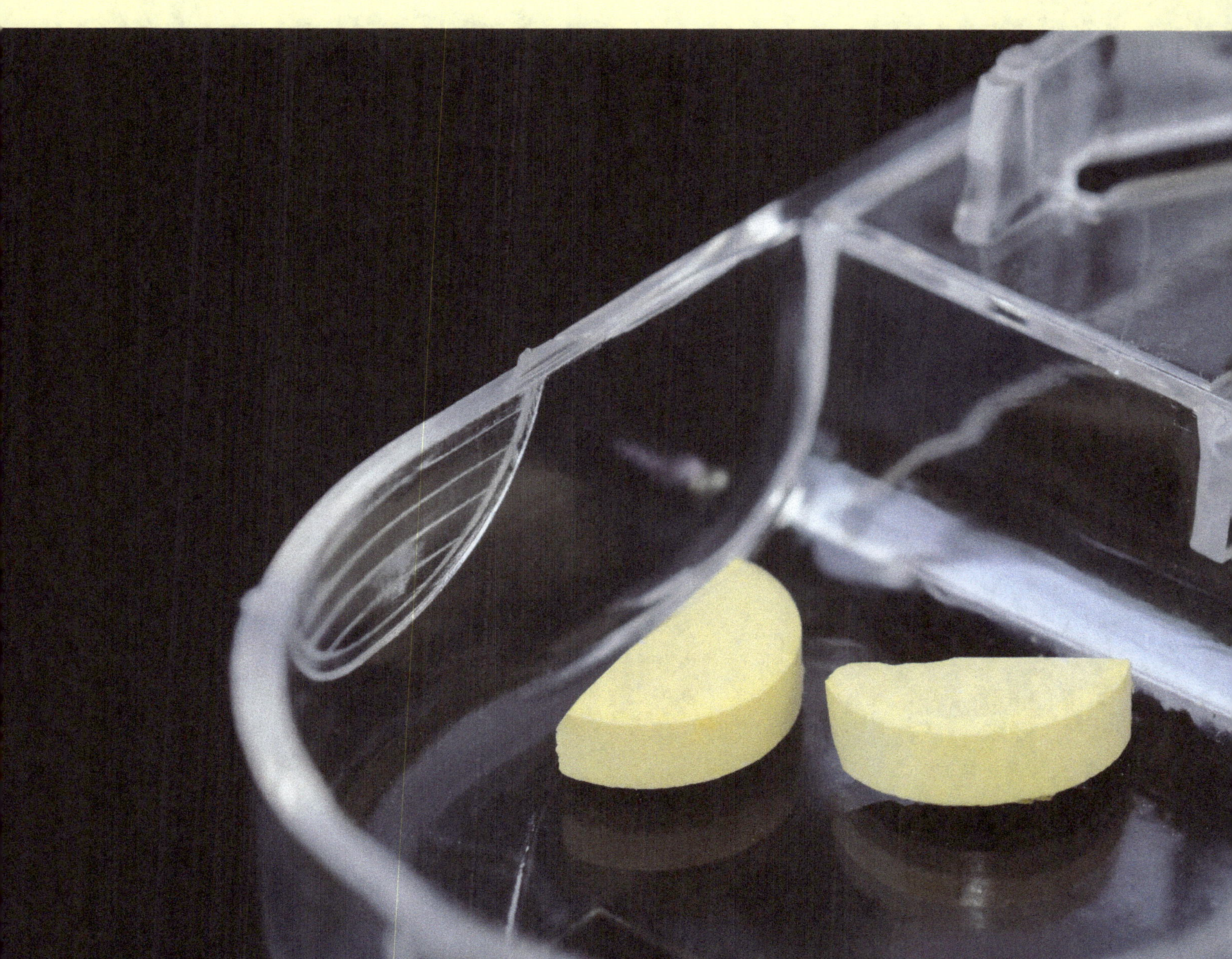

Turn it upside down and place it with the cap facing the ground. Step back a few yards.

If you did everything right, about 6 to 10 seconds later you'll hear a loud pop and your rocket will launch 10 to 20 feet skyward!

BE CAREFUL: If it doesn't launch, wait a couple of minutes before picking up the film holder. It probably means you didn't put the cap on tightly enough so the pressurized gas leaked out.

THE SCIENCE BEHIND IT:

When you added the water to the tablet it began to dissolve and created a gas—carbon dioxide. As the gas is formed, it needs a lot more space so it creates a build-up of pressure inside the plastic holder. After a few seconds, the pressure is so great that the cap is blasted downward and the "rocket" flies up. This is the same process of thrust that's used when a real rocket goes up into space except it uses rocket fuel.

EXPERIMENT 4

MONSTER MARSHMALLOW

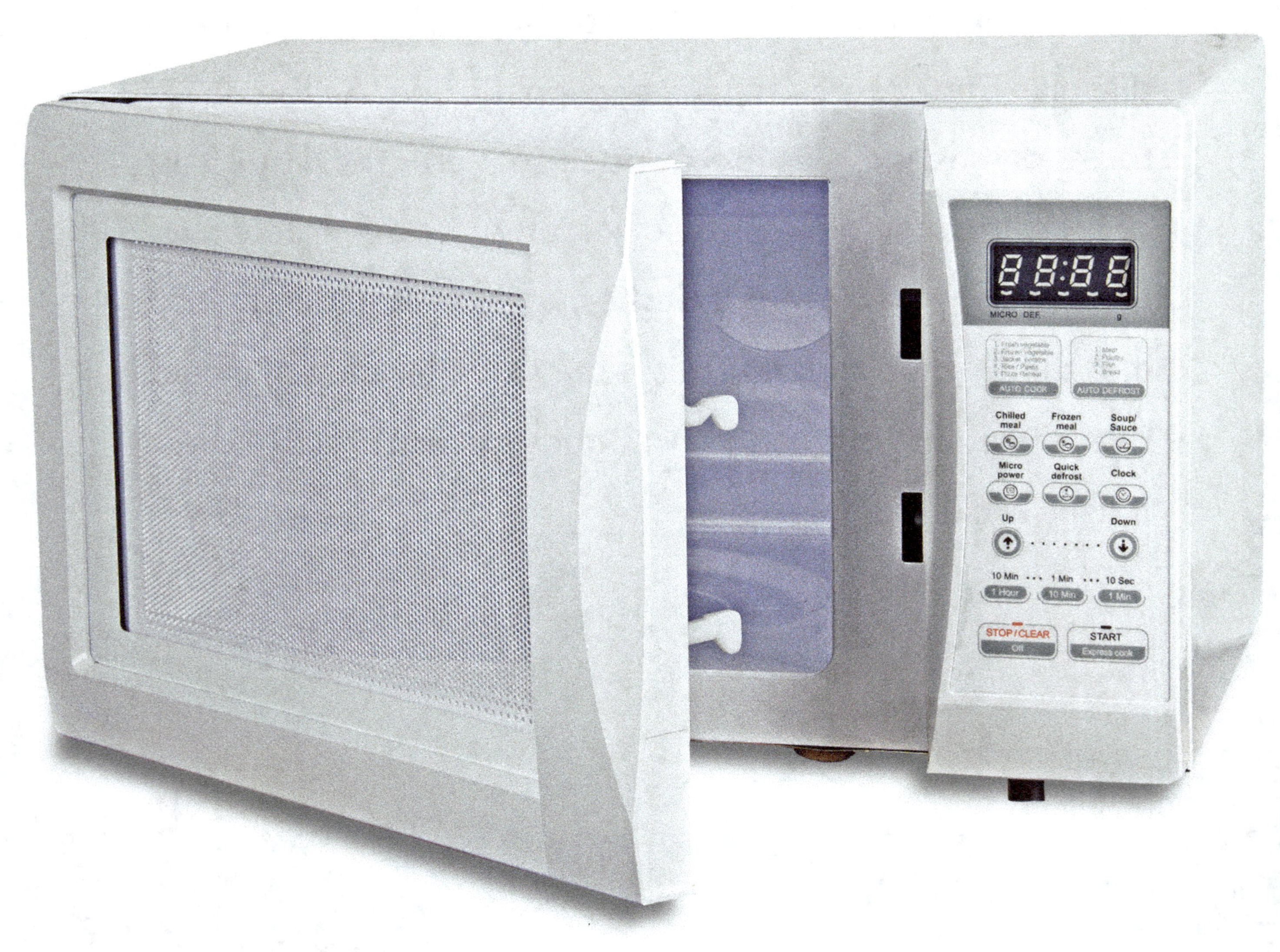

THINGS YOU'LL NEED:

You'll need a microwave oven. You'll need a bag of large marshmallows. You'll also need a plate. Food coloring is optional if you want to draw a face on your marshmallow for fun.

WHAT TO DO:

STEP 1

Place a large marshmallow on a plate. Draw a face on it if you want to.

STEP 2

Have an adult help you put the marshmallow in the microwave.

:30
HEALTHY COOKING
Thai Menu
Quick Meal
Defrost
Microwave
Deodorizer
Child Lock
Stop /Ene

Set the microwave for 30 seconds, start the microwave, and watch what happens to your marshmallow. It's becoming a monster!

Take the marshmallow out. Be careful because it will be very hot!

Try this experiment for different amounts of time and note your findings on a chart.

THE SCIENCE BEHIND IT:

You probably know this already but marshmallows are mostly composed of sugar mixed with water surrounding bubbles of air. That's what makes marshmallows so soft. When you microwave your marshmallow, the microwave gets the water molecules in the marshmallow very excited and they vibrate quickly. The hot water molecules inside the marshmallow heat the sugar up, which softens it. The hot water molecules also warm up the trapped air bubbles.

When you heat up the air in a container that is closed, which is your marshmallow in this case, the molecules of gas start moving faster and faster and they push against the outside walls of the marshmallow.

пароварка
СВЧ
рецепт

This process makes the marshmallow expand like crazy! If it puffs up and expands too much, some of the bubbles of air will burst and the marshmallow will deflate just as if it were a deflated balloon.

When you take the marshmallow out of the microwave, eventually it will cool down. The bubbles will shrink and the sugar will get hard. That's due to the fact that some of the water evaporated out of the marshmallow when it was heated up. The cooled-down marshmallow gets very dry and crunchy.

If you zap your marshmallow in the microwave for too long it might turn brown or black on the inside. That's because the sugar has caramelized just like it does when you hold a marshmallow over a campfire.

SUMMARY

Things that explode are fun! Chemical reactions can be dangerous though so make sure you work with an adult whenever you perform experiments at home or at school.

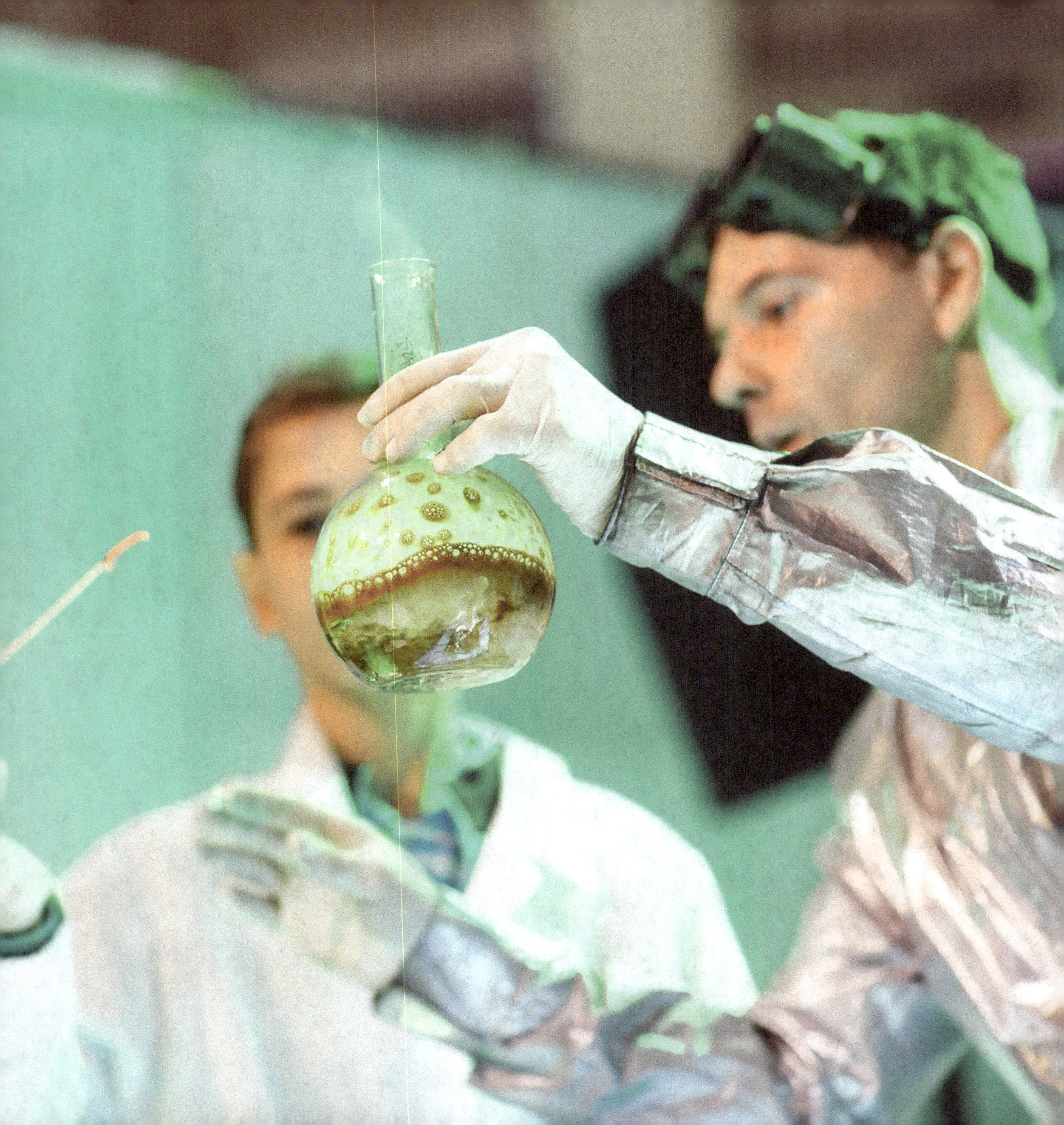

Once you set up your experiment you should form a hypothesis and use your experiment to determine whether your hypothesis is correct. By coming up with a hypothesis and performing your experiment to test it, you're using the scientific method.

Awesome! Now that you've done these exploding science experiments you may want to do some experiments with food in the Baby Professor book Food Experiments for Would-Be Scientists: Food Book for Children.

Visit

BABY PROFESSOR
EDUCATION KIDS

www.BabyProfessorBooks.com
to download Free Baby Professor eBooks
and view our catalog of new and exciting
Children's Books